Let's Start A Cult

The Power of Radical Belief

Braxton Amundson

Let's Start A Cult
The Power of Radical Belief

ISBN: 978-0-578-59229-9

TABLE OF CONTENTS

INTRODUCTION

"Follow me, and I will make
you Fishers of Men."

—Jesus Christ

"A cult is bullshit. It's created by one
person and that person knows it's
bullshit! In a Religion...that
dude is dead."

—Joe Rogan

It's Saturday. I'm out to lunch with my friends having normal conversation—well normal for me. We're talking deep philosophy, life, my friends are sharing their vision and I'm digging into the part that connects to their heart. "Do you understand the difference between a vision and a goal? You're telling me your what and your how. I'm not interested in your what and your how. I want to know you WHY! Your what and your how are your vehicles. I'm not making them wrong, they're inherently beautiful. You effectively have a $6 billion dollar rocket ship that can get you to anywhere in the universe, but without a WHY that rocket ship has no fuel." My friends dig in and tell me their WHY. They dig into the world they want to create and the purpose behind it. It's real. I feel each one of them.

Shortly afterwards, the waiter comes to bring us the check and clean off the table, and my friends and I go outside to ride motorized scooters through town to sightsee. As I walk outside, a man in his 50's follows me out and taps me on the shoulder.

"I couldn't help but overhear you coaching your clients. (HA!! He thinks my friends are my clients!!!!) That was amazing. I want to hire you to speak at one of my company trainings. My name is Jamal, and I own a mortgage company. How much does it cost to book you?"

(I've literally never booked a paid speaking gig my entire life at this point)

"It's $10,000 for the first booking, and $6,500 for every booking after that."

"Great! Here's my card. Call me this week. I would love to book you at our next event."

My initial reaction: WHAT THE FUCK JUST HAPPENED?!?!

My next reaction: BRAXTON!!!!! WHY DIDN'T YOU SAY $50,000 YOU IDIOT!!!!

We are the creators of our reality. What we believe to be true will become true. The invitation I make to each and every person is to choose your beliefs such that they are congruent with the most empowering context. Energy goes where energy flows.

You see, getting amazing offers isn't anything more than an average, ordinary day for me. Things like this happen every day that I wake up and get out of bed. They happen to you, too, but if you aren't present to what's happening around you, you don't see it. It will fly right over your head. When you're worried about how you're going to pay next months mortgage, you miss out on the opportunity to pay off your entire house. I'm not talking about a raise at work. Raises are bullshit. Fuck raises. I'm talking about a revolution baby.

Garrain Jones, a mentor of mine, took time on Saturday to pour into me. I had to learn to get out of my head and into my heart. He got me from a place of complacency to a place of commitment, from surface level to deep. After leaving his house, I thanked him for going there with me. He looked me dead in the eye—I'll never forget it—and said, "Braxton, the best way to say 'Thank you' is to apply what you learned and pay it forward." This writing is me doing just that. This is me saying 'Thank You' to everyone who taught me such valuable lessons.

Now, let's first be crystal clear about this: when I say, "Let's Start a Cult," I'm not trying to win you over and create a religion called "Braxtonism" or anything like that...yet. To me, a "Cult" is a movement in which followers become raving fans committed to growing the following of the founder's vision through a set of common beliefs and philosophies.

When it comes to Radical Belief, I will many times refer to Jesus Christ as he has set the bar for what it looks like to break through any belief barrier. If life were a video game, Jesus Christ is easily the highest scoring player of all time. How did he accomplish what he accomplished? Very simple, he believed he could. Jesus said, "If you had faith the size of a mustard seed, you could say to a mountain 'jump' and it would jump."

Before we jump into this any further, let's first define what I mean by 'belief.' Our actions define what we believe in. There is a huge difference between understanding something and truly believing it. The Law of Pendulum states that an object released in a pendulum will never go higher than the original point unless there are external forces acting upon this law. Make enough sense? Simple enough to understand? Now, let's see if you believe it. Imagine you are standing on top of a chair, and I hold a 100 lb cannonball suspended by a steel wire up to your nose; then I say, "The Law of Pendulum states that an object released in a pendulum will never go higher than its original point unless there are external forces acting upon it." Though you may fully understand this law; my guess is whenever the cannon ball starts getting closer and closer to your face, your belief will waiver and you will move out of the way. In life, it's important to BOTH understand AND believe the concepts. Where else in your life are you jumping out of the way when you are otherwise safe?

Another example I like to use when it comes to Radical belief is bees. I watched the Bee Movie and it began with this quote: "According to all known laws of aviation, there is no way that a bee should be able to fly. Its wings are too small to get its fat little body off the ground. The bee, of course, flies anyways. Because bees don't care what humans think is impossible." This really hit home for me. What do you want to do that you have told yourself is impossible? What have you done that was seemingly impossible that became the daily norm? If I told someone 100 years ago that I could pull a rectangular box out of my pocket, press a few buttons on it and in a matter of a few seconds I could be having a face to face conversation with someone on the other side of the world, people would think that was crazy! But today, we do it and think nothing of it.

For a long time, I struggled with a weight issue. I wasn't fat by any means, but I was certainly a bit overweight. For a long time, I always believed that I was a slightly overweight guy. I thought that's just the cards that I was dealt. I was a guy who worked out, lifted weights and ate chicken wings and hamburgers. When I changed my habits, my beliefs changed rapidly, and I lost 20 lbs in 6 weeks. What resonated with me is the fact that my habits were not in congruence with what I wanted. I wanted a trim body, but I continued with my daily habits. Einstein defined insanity as doing the same thing over and over again and expecting different results. I was living insanity. I realize now with the benefit of hindsight that if I want my life to change, I get to be the change. When you decide that you are worth it, the universe always responds.

In this book,we will discuss the elements of radical belief. The elements are as follows:

Intention, connection, Style Flex, interruption, charisma and trust.

How did a 28 year old from small town Punxsutawney, PA raised by two devout Christians get to a place where he is all of a sudden theorizing about immortality and creating polarizing beliefs that cause massive uproar? Honestly, I am not exactly sure, but I am happy to share my story with you, and maybe you can send me a DM on Instagram (shameless plug: follow @braxxonbraxx) and let me know your theory. All I know is that the set of beliefs that I have adapted over the years have been labeled 'polarizing' and 'controversial', but those who have adapted such beliefs and have chosen to live by them have created extraordinary results in their lives. I am not trying to tell you what to believe or give you THE Truth, but from what I believe, whatever we choose to be true becomes true in our reality, so why not believe in whatever belief makes you the author of your own life?

Born into a Cult

I was born in small town in Punxsutawney, PA. Yes, I know what you're thinking, that is the home of Punxsutawney Phil Seer of Seers, Sage of Sages, Prognosticator of Prognosticators, and Weather Prophet Extraordinary; and yes, I am very proud to say this anytime someone asks. I was raised by two very loving Christian parents who did the absolute best to raise me to live out the Word of God and be a good Christian. When I was in 8th grade, I attended a small Christian school all the way through Middle School and was even a state Bible Quiz champion. The beauty of being raised in this environment is that I adapted a strong set of morals and values implemented in me at a very young age, but as we all know through Newton's 3rd Law 'For every action there is an equal and opposite reaction' and not to say there is a right or wrong way to raise a child, the sheltered environment that I grew up in created a rebellious state in me when I was 'Thrown out into the scary world of the Punxsutawney Public School System' (this is a joke if you didn't catch it).

I was by no means a 'bad' kid, quite contrary. I just had a need to question every idea and belief that was brought to my attention. Like a little kid, I always wanted to know 'why.' In elementary school, I, all of a sudden, wasn't allowed to play Pokemon because Pokemon evolved and in the Christian home, evolution is like bad and stuff, nor was I allowed to watch or read Harry Potter because of Wizardry and Witchcraft which is supposedly Satanic or something. I respected my mother's wishes, but deep down inside of me always questioned where the line is drawn between being true to one's beliefs and having fun with fantasy.

What I really wanted more than anything was independence. I wanted the freedom to trust myself and make my own choices. When I was 21 years old, I was approached by a man named Dave Kleifgen to join a summer sales and leadership program called Southwestern Advantage--a door-to-door company the provides an at home learning system for kids from below school age to high school seniors preparing for college. I attended an informational session and loved what he had to say. It was a direct sales opportunity to build skills and character to help young people achieve their goals in life through positive attitude, goal setting, persistence, and integrity. It was said to be cut throat and about 30% of the people who start out don't make it past their 3rd or 4th week. To me, this sounded amazing. I was finally given the chance to compete on a level playing field and receive an honest look at how I show up. I left the info session fired up! I called my parents, and they didn't share the same excitement. "You are going to sell books halfway across the country door-to-door? How did you meet this guy? Shouldn't you be doing something that in your field of study?" I always had a deep trust in myself and my intuition to guide me to where I get to go, and over time, I won my parents approval. I began meeting with Dave weekly and my friends started to ask questions about the legitimately of what I was doing. "I heard it's a scam! I read online that it's a cult! Why don't you stay here and party over the summer?" My immediate response was to laugh at this. It's funny and ironic because these are the same friends who before this would laugh at people for believing everything they read online... now they are those people. May came around and I was off to sales school. I left inspired and headed to Oklahoma. I DEFINITELY see how this might be considered to be cult-like. We were constantly asked to stretch out of our comfort zones and drop our 'cool card.' Each morning we would dance around in the parking lot of our break-fast place and make complete fools of ourselves in public. It was slightly embarrassing and incredibly fun. The cult-like tendencies weren't necessarily a bad thing, but when one embarks on a journey of personal growth, he or she must be bought in 100% or it just won't work. 100% is easy; everything else is hard. **The degree of skepticism I have towards what I am doing is the degree that I am away from achieving my goal.**

Southwestern taught me to be bought in 100% and fully committed to what I set out to do. The concept of future success pending on my level of belief was presented to me in this culture. Integrity is when our actions and words align. Understanding a concept is simple, but believing the concept takes mastery. The man I will one day be, I am now becoming. If I don't commit and dive into what I'm doing in this present moment, how will I fully committed and dive into things later in life? These principles made complete sense to me logically and conceptually; but as a human being with 21 years of bad habits, my words did not always align with my actions. There were times that summer where I was off schedule and wasting time. There were times where my attitude wasn't to a place where I was 100% bought in. Despite the trials and tribulations that I endured, I finished the summer in the top 5% of the 3,000 first year dealers and was excited to move into a manager role. After 2 more summers of personal growth through direct sales, I was ready to take my new found skillset and enhanced character out into the world. At 23 years old, I started my own business buying and selling college textbooks.

I became an entrepreneur completely by accident. After college, I was on a road trip across the country when I ran out of money and needed to find a way to make quick cash before I could come home. Not wanting to have to ask my dad for money, I began searching for ways to make money on my own. I found out that college professors are given books for free as marketing by the publisher. I was in Bloomington, IN, and I ended up going to Indiana University and began asking professors for their unwanted books and took them down to the bookstore in exchange for cash. To my surprise, this was much easier to do than I thought. I counted up my money at the end of the day and had $822. I decided to try it a few more days at a few other nearby college such as Indiana State University, Eastern Illinois University, and IU Southeast and in my first week made almost $3500. I came home and enrolled several of my friends to join me and scaled my business by buying a warehouse in my hometown and enrolled my retired father to do my inventory and ship out orders, selling the books retail online and paying myself and my friends out wholesale.

Over the years, I made decent money right out of college and managed it very carefully. At 25 years old, I was doing over $1 Million in revenue, owned 2 homes and was making close to $200k/year in profit from this business. I began working with several of my friends as well and taught them the 'cult-like' principles that I had learned at

Southwestern. Though I had financial and career success, I didn't feel fulfilled in the work that I was doing. I became careless in my behavior and began acting out as a cry for help. I was doing cocaine practically every day during my work day to fill the void of what I was missing in life. I was trying to live the 'eccentric millionaire' baller lifestyle that one might identify with from watching the *Wolf of Wall Street*. I would take weekend trips to Amsterdam and other places across Europe to try and find joy and fulfillment. Nothing ever came to heart until shortly after my 26th birthday, I received a call from my friend Lester.

Lester was always an interesting character to say the least. He was the epitome of an interruption. Kind of like a male Lady Gaga, he always would throw curveballs to keep people on their toes. There were times where I literally believed that he believed he was the 2nd coming of Jesus Christ. When it comes to starting a Cult, Lester is the guy. The first time I met the man, I was sitting in the basement of Irving's cafe at Penn State University. My friend Dave wanted to introduce me to his sales manager, Lester. He was hyped up and Dave went up to get us coffee as Lester sat down at the table. He was 300lbs and stared at me with crazy eyes for what seemed like 10 minutes (in all reality, it was probably about 3).

He breaks the silence by saying, "Braxton, do you think I'm attractive?"

Not wanting to hurt his feelings while simultaneously trying to sound smart, I danced around the question, "Everyone is attractive in their own way…"

"Braxton, I don't work with liars. Do you think I'm attractive?" He replied

"Beauty is in the eye of the beholder…"

"Braxton, I'm not attractive. I'm 300 lbs. My name is Lester," he reaches for his bag to pull out a magazine. He then flips it open to a United Airlines commercial with a beautiful model dressed as a flight attendant, "but this is a picture of my wife. If you work with me, I'll teach you how to marry up in life." Drops the mic and walks away. That's Lester.

JOINING A CULT

Lester and I always had our run ins over the next few years. I remained single and always jokingly (or not so jokingly) reminded him about how he had promised to teach me how to marry up in life. He was always an incredibly supportive friend and his life philosophies always blew my mind.

"Braxton, remember the time where I told you that I would teach you how to marry up in life?"

"Umm… yes. You mean like 7 years ago…"

"I found it, Braxton. I found it! You gotta come to Los Angeles and take this workshop!"

"Fuck it! I'll go!"

He sends me a link to the Mastery in Transformational Training (MITT) website. At this point, I had heard about MITT for quite some time and have had dozens of friends go through the process and create amazing results in their lives. I, in fact, had wanted to go for years, but didn't really know how to get involved and, at this stage in my life, I sure as hell wasn't about to show vulnerability and humanness by asking.

This is where my real journey began. I ended up signing up for the Basic training in May because the summers are a bit slower for my business. I was excited. I, however, had absolutely no idea what I was about to get myself into— my whole life was about to flip and turn upside down. It is really interesting though, I have been around the Mastery in Transformational Training community for quite some time and at this point have enrolled over 50 of my friends and family into the training. Something I say that I truly stand behind is this: "Your journey starts the second you put skin in the game." Once I signed up is when I started questioning everything that I've been doing myself. It had me asking myself about my purpose and what really brings me fulfillment. I hadn't stepped foot into the training and was already starting to question my life.

May came around and I stepped into the training. **I WAS FREAKED OUT!** My initial reaction: this is a cult. My next thought, "I was baited here with a $500 admission ticket so they can sell me the more expensive courses." or "Wow! They are pressuring me to give my word and then they are using it against me. This is controlling. This is manipulation. I don't like this.I didn't want to complete this program in the slightest. I didn't trust anyone and I didn't want to be there. I was in from out of town, I decided that I would just go and hang with a friend for the rest of the weekend until my flight back home. I called him up, "Hey Jonny! Lester invited me to another cult, and I don't want to do this one." He told me he had plans on Thursday but I was welcome to hang out for the rest of the weekend. Begrudgingly, I went back for the second day. That is when things started to open up for me. The Bible says, "and now we see things as a reflection as if looking in a mirror" 1 Corinthians 13:12.I. This course was a mirror reflection for how I was living my life. I didn't trust anyone because at the time, I was not trustworthy. I was experiencing control and manipulation because I was practicing controlling and manipulative tactics. It has absolutely nothing to do with the trainer, the course or my peers and everything to do with me and how I was showing up. I called my friend back the next day and told him that I decided to complete the program, and I invited him to my graduation on Sunday. Two years later, I am now leading the leadership program in which he is enrolled in as a student. What opened up for me in doing this work has changed my life. I am able to take responsibility for everything that happens in my life. I live from the mind space 'if it's to be, it's up to me.' That isn't just a catch phrase, that is exactly how I choose to live my life every single day. I am in full ownership of everything that happens in the world around me. I come from the mindset that I created the world around me and everything in the world I have manifested and called forth to teach me a lesson. Life happens for me, not to me. It wasn't easy looking in the mirror, but it gave me my power back. I have become a master of seeing through walls of people and into their greatness. When I evoke someone's vision and call them forth into transformation, I can see exactly what has stopped them from achieving everything they have ever dreamed of up until now. Whatever it is that I am resisting in further development myself is what I am resisting in all areas of my life. When I invite my friends and family to come with me on my journey, there are really only 3 reasons why someone wouldn't join me on my mission:

1. **A lack of trust**. Personally, this is my favorite to work through because it typically involves us looking back at our relationship and finding out where the trust has been broken, Clearing the event and moving forward. It takes responsibility and being in the ownership of what took place and committing

to exactly who I will be moving forward. It takes courage to open up and own what happened. Once the trust is recreated we can move our relationship forward and it is built back up to a place stronger than before. A perfect example of a lack of trust: someone told me that they read reviews of the program online and it's definitely not for me. I read all of the experiences that people have been having and this just doesn't seem like something I would do. How I respond to this: typically, your experience in programs like this is a direct reflection of how you experience the person who invited you to it. If your experience of me is a cult leader--which it certainly should be--then you will experience a cult. If you trust me, there is nothing stopping you from having an amazing experience.

2. **Money Conversations** are typically a reflection of one's self worth. When I invest into myself, I am symbolically saying, "I am worth it. I trust myself enough to create the value in what I am given.' lots of times, an investment in oneself is the hardest investment to make because it involves being responsible in creating the value and believing in oneself wholeheartedly. The question I ask here is, "What is your vision?" I then dig deep to find the world this person is truly committed to creating. When the vision is strong enough, it is clear that it can't be accomplished alone. I then ask, "If that is the world

you are creating, is that something you can achieve on your own? Well of you aren't willing to invest in yourself, how can you expect others to invest in you?" In 2018, I took time to go see Tony Robbins' Unleash the Power Within in New York City. I was so inspired that I signed up for his entire program that included: Unleash the Power Within, Business Mastery, Date with Destiny, Life and Wealth Mastery and a 4 month coaching program. I spent a total of $15,000,* and I paid in full to be bumped up to diamond seating at the next UPW event. When I went back home my mom asked me about the event. I told her how amazing and inspired I was from it and that I couldn't wait to go to the rest of the courses that I signed up for. She cautiously asked me how much it cost. When I told her it was $15,000 she replied, "Braxton Benson Franklin Amundson, that is a lot of money! Why would you spend that much money?" In which i replied, "because I want to hang out with people who don't think it's a lot of money." My dad chimes in "Well... He has a point..." My point: $15,000 is only a lot of money when I say so. When I see it as a small price to pay to live the life I truly desire, then I open up the possibility of creating unlimited earning potential. Again, an investment in myself is symbolic of me telling myself, 'im worth it. When I believe in myself, people will follow suit in believing in me.

3. **Lack of Time conversation** People who resist growing because of time are typically lacking intimacy in their lives because they get so caught up in the 'doing' that they lose presence being with the ones they love. I had a friend who called me and told me that he lives the work but it was happening at an extremely inconvenient time in his life. I asked him if he was open to hearing my perspective. He said 'yes' and I responded 'Thank God Martin Luther King wasn't waiting for the right time to have a dream. Thank God Jackie Robinson wasn't waiting for the right time to be the first black baseball player. Jackie Robinson entered the major leagues are arguably the worst time for a black man. Leaderships to wait for the right time, it chooses the right person.' if not now, when? If not you, who? My vision is not going to happen on its own. Standing as the source, it is up to me to create the time to achieve it because if I don't have the time to achieve my vision, I can't possibly expect anyone else to have the time for it.

STUDENT BECOMES MASTER

Enrollment is the ability to obtain a following. When one is practicing Radical Belief, he/she is fueled to share this with every single person he/she comes across. Enrollment happens when one creates trust and intimacy. When

I Radically believe in the mission that I'm on, I give the people who I'm enrolling 3 choices:

1. Join me on my mission.
2. Stop talking to me
3. Enroll me on why proceeding and alternative direction better serves the overall vision

We as human beings are born to connect and relate. It is what we crave and the more intimate we become, the more capable we are to both love and be loved. Here's a quote from my all time favorite book *The Alchemist*, "When you love, you always strive to become better than you are." We were born to grow. We either grow together or we fall apart. Intimacy is the ability to see people for who they authentically are and speak those ways of being into existence.

In order to Start a Cult, one must become a Master enroller. The following chapters, I will share my steps to master to create the following for your Cult (or business or whatever other thing you want to call it).

THE NEW TESTAMENT: LAYING THE GROUNDWORK

Life happens for me, not to me."

—Tony Robbins

Everything in life is an absolute blessing when I choose to see it. We as human beings are given gifts of trials and tribulations so that we can fully appreciate the joys in life. When living life open heartedly, feelings are magnified. I invite you to fall in love with all parts of the journey as God gives us mountains and valleys to strengthen us. Transformation happens when the heart is opened to everything. Happiness is a choice and I choose to be happy no matter the circumstance because if I am breathing, that is reason enough to be grateful.

One of the biggest lessons I've learned in life is that of gratitude. I have found that only when I am grateful for what I have in front of me do I receive my next level. Whether it be money or relationships or health, gratitude in the present creates joy and abundance.

I am blessed with one of the best mentors in life in Garrain Jones who has been like a big brother to me since I met him. In a conversation with him, he dug into what it means to be gratitude, "You can't have $1,000 if you don't appreciate the $100 you have right now." Since then, I've dug into this phrase and applied it everywhere else in my life.

I am unbelievably blessed with so much in life, but when I am focused on what I don't have, I am in turn throwing shade on everything in front of me. I have both done this to people AND have had this done to me. I was at a friend's surprise birthday party and she came to me and was opening up about how she was upset that a few of her friends weren't there. I asked her if I could point something out and she said I could. I said, "As someone who is here, I feel like my presence isn't good enough when I took the time to come to your party only to hear you complain about who didn't show up. I do this in my life, as well, so I'm also saying this for myself. Look around. There are dozens of people here to celebrate you. I invite you to appreciate all of them."

There are so many other areas that this applies, but the bottom line is be grateful for what is in front of you. Then and only then can we receive more. The wanting of more is always going to be there, but I have trained my mind to focus on the present and what is available for me right now rather than to wish for the future.

Everything in life happens for a reason. In reading the Tao te Ching, I learned that there is no love without pain because having the pains of life is what gives me an appreciation for its joys and bliss. Life throws me challenges only when I am strong enough to face them. I am blessed with trials and tribulations because those prepare me for my next level. I have learned to be grateful for the pain because it means I am alive. It is natural to close off and try to avoid painful times through drugs, alcohol, surface level conversations, putting up a façade, etc.; but the only way out is through and understanding that when the work is done, the next level of joy and bliss awaits on the other side.

In the summer of 2019, I experienced one of the most tragic moments in my life: my sister-in-law was found dead in her kayak in the ocean. At the time, I was living in LA., My brother and his wife in Florida, and my parents in Pennsylvania. I booked the next flight out to be with family. I found out in the morning, but didn't get a flight out until late at night. That moment, sitting alone devastated in my apartment was horrifying. I just wanted a hug. I just wanted to be with someone. I didn't know where to go, so I drove to the MITT community office. Never in my entire life have I felt so supported by so many people. My cup was filled up by so many shoulders to lean on;when I got to my family, I had so much more to give.

I was standing with my brother in his moments of grief. I told him it's important to feel the pain because that's what heals. I told him that I was there for anything he needs and I told him in moments like this, I always remind myself that on the other side is something beautiful.

Take the story of Job in the Bible, as an example. Job had an amazing life complete with wealth and a beautiful, loving family. Everything in his life on paper seemed to be great, until one day Job lost everything. He lost all of his kids, his wife, his health and all of his money. In this moment, Job had a choice, he could sit and feel sorry for himself, or he could feel the pain, understand that these are tough times, grieve for the time being and choose to move forward.

When Job chose to surrender and give thanks to God and trust that God will always provide, God gave him and even greater life than he had before. He blessed him with an amazing wife, more beautiful children, better health and even greater wealth than he ever had. This story taught me to trust that even in the darkest moments, God will always provide, but first it takes gratitude for every single moment and trusting that on the other side is the next level of life.

THE NEW TESTAMENT: ALWAYS BE GRATEFUL

"Leaders see obstacles as opportunities"

—Michael Strasner

I have found that strength and power happen when we see our greatest challenges as opportunities to grow. I have become a master of the transition and have made a reputation for myself in becoming one of the best coaches in guiding people through the transition process.

In 2016, I had a friend who I was trying to enroll into my business for quite some time. I knew I had a better opportunity available for him than what he currently had; but many are fearful to choose change. Most change occurs during a time that is either sink or swim, and I didn't create within him the urgency to change. However, one day, he was arrested for DUI and fired from his workplace. When I picked him up from the police station, looked him in the eye and said, "I'm going to make this the best thing that's ever happened to you." He immediately began working with me and growing himself to a place where he was better than before. Everything is an opportunity if I choose to see it that way.

CONNECT WITH VISION

"Leaders have a powerful vision."

—Michael Strasner

I always say to myself, "My vision and my commitments are greater than my thoughts and my feelings." My commitment to my vision is my North Star. When my vision is tested, I find myself battling my thoughts and feelings that, at times, try to diverge me from manifesting my vision. I sometimes don't feel like stretching myself. I sometimes don't feel like pushing into the unknown, but the vision that I am committed to creating is a world where everyone knows that they matter where every voice is heard, every face is seen and people feel safe to express themselves and feel warmly received when doing to. What I am offering is a set of tools that give people the ability to cultivate meaningful relationships that mutually move one another forward. My vision is so much bigger than my feelings and will only manifest when I stay connected to it and push through the thoughts that arise that slow me down.

Bob Marley is one of the biggest visionary musicians of all time. His music speaks of peace, forgiveness and prosperity that this world so desperately needs. His commitment to his vision was beyond comprehension and what I am about to share is but a mere speck in what he went through to send his message.

Bob Marley had a concert prepared to share his message on the biggest platform. It was set to air on television, and he viewed it as his biggest opportunity to make the biggest difference that he possibly could. The night before the concert, however, he was shot several times and rushed to the emergency room. While the doctor was operating on him, he kept urging him to stitch him up so he could perform the next day. The doctor said he would do everything that he could to get him back to strength but there was no way that he would ever recommend that he perform. Bob, however, was resilient. The doctor took out the bullets, stitched him up and the next day, he delivered the greatest performance of his lifetime. When asked after the show what drives him to continue, Bob Marley said one of the most powerful quotes of all time, "The people who were trying to make this world worse are not taking a day off. Why should I?"

I think we can all take a page out of Bob Marley's playbook. I am sure that Bob Marley didn't feel like performing. I'm sure that he felt like laying in bed and recovering, but nobody understood more than he did that one's vision and one's commitment are so much greater than the momentary thoughts and feelings. What is possible in your life when you are connected to a vision that strong?

"Fight for your life, not your survival."

—Michael Strasner

I was in a place where I was grieving the pain of someone very close to me when a friend called to ask how I was doing. Knowing that I create the reality that I live in through my words and my mindset, I responded, "I am blessed to have cultivated a mindset where I can turn what seems to be the most unfortunate events into life's greatest blessings."

I say many of these things on the fly. Not because I'm trying to sound smart or profound, but because I REFUSE to give energy to anything that doesn't serve me. Instead of saying that I am struggling with something, I say that I am blessed with a challenge that serves as an opportunity to grow. It is the small shifts in language that creates a massive impact on how I see the world. Positivity is powerful. Events are neutral, how I choose to interpret the events is what creates my reality. **The extent of the interpretation by which I turn experience into language and beauty into emotion is the vastness of joy in my life.**

BOOK OF BRAXTON

CHAPTER 1

INTENTION

"Rock, Paper, Scissors: A Game if intention or a game of chance?"

—Keith Bentz

Intention is powerful and is the foundation for enrollment. A strong intention comes with closing all of the back doors and having the eyes on the prize. In 1519, when Hernan Cortes first landed in Mexico, his army was incredibly outnumbered by the Aztecs. Many of the soldiers were ready to get back on the ships and head back to Spain as they appeared to be outmatched, but Cortes instead ordered the ships to be burnt so there was no other choice but to take Mexico by storm. For Cortes, there was no back door. There was no option to surrender. He created an environment of 'kill or be killed.' Just like a marriage 'Until death do us part.' It doesn't say until death do us part OR the Aztec army slaughters too many of our people. It doesn't say 'Until death do us part OR we want to return home to our families. Cortes dropped the possibility of 'OR' and manifested his intention.

To create a strong intention, one must find the value for himself/herself in 'burning the boats.' One must be sure that it is something that is 100% worth committing to and create leverage. "What will life be like when I manifest my intention?" "What are the prices that I would be paying if I backed out and didn't manifest my intention?"

In the movie Braveheart, Mel Gibson's character William Wallace is leading the Scottish army into battle in their fight for their independence—their freedom—something that almost everyone values at an exceptionally high rate. They are outnumbered and outgunned and many of the soldiers want to turn around, go back home, and live the rest of their lives under the rule of the English. Though his men were defeated, Wallace knew what it was like to go into battle with a clear intention and purpose behind it.

"Sons of Scotland, I am William Wallace"

(Crowd mocks him) "William Wallace is 7 feet tall"

"Yes I've heard, killed men by the hundreds, and if here were here today he would defeat the English with bolts of lightning from his eyes and balls of Fire from his ass"

(Crowd laughs)

"I am William Wallace," he continues, "and what I see is a whole army of my countrymen in defiance of tyranny. You have come here as free men, and free men you are. What will you do without freedom. Will you fight."

(A voice in the crowd) "Fight? Against that? No, we will run, and will will live

"Aye, fight and you may die. Run… and you'll live—at least for a while. And dying in your bed, many years from now—are you willing to trade all of those days from this day 'til that for one chance—JUST ONE CHANCE—to tell our enemies that they may take their lives but they'll never take OUR FREEDOM!!!!!

(Crowd cheers outrageously)

Now that you are clear on what you will be doing and why you're doing it and the why is now so strong that it is time to make a powerful declaration—the last part of creating a strong intention.

Declaration starts with language. Language indicates the level of commitment. The levels are as follows:

1. Resistant: "I won't do it and you can't make me"
2. Committed until "I will try my best"

3. Conditionally Committed "I will do it if…"
4. Committed "I will make it happen. You can count on me"

Everyone knows that in America, the day that we recognize our Independence as a nation is July 4th, 1776. The thing I find most inspiring about the Fourth of July is that it isn't the day we "won our independence" after a war—it is the day we declared ourselves free from someone else's nonsense and then mutually pledged our "lives, fortunes, and sacred honor" in support of this declaration.

In other words, we said, "We are free; right now", and decided--no matter what it takes, we're going to live into this truth we've spoken (declared) until everyone else agrees that it's true.

When that type of courage and integrity combo shows up in the world it seems the universe becomes plastic and bends, making the impossible happen.

Submitting to someone else's nonsense because we are afraid of how much it will cost or what we may lose isn't really patriotic.

"That's just the way it is" in 1776 means no hot dogs and fireworks for us today.

It's patriotic to make an outrageous declaration about something radically pro-human being possible, no matter the odds, and then doing whatever it takes to have our actions align with the truth we've spoken.

The war with England ended in 1783. Our Independence Day is July 4th, 1776. We are free because we declared it and lived in it.

Tony Robbins says, "In life, you get what you tolerate." I choose to hold myself to the highest level of commitment which creates trust and leads to integrity. When I am in integrity, Magic happens and the world aligns. Like I said earlier, 100% is easy, everything else is hard. My vision is for everyone to know that they matter. For every voice to be heard and for every person to be seen. My vision is for everyone to freely express themselves and open their hearts to reach their fullest potential. When I keep my word and follow through with the things that I say I'm going to do, I communicate with the person 'You Matter.' When I don't, what I'm communicating is 'I don't care enough about you to keep my commitment to you. You don't matter to me. Something came up that was more important to me than keeping my word with you." Extreme? Maybe, but there is a certain truth to it, and I will prove it.

If I were the President of the United States, or Tom Cruise, or whoever else you looked up to, and we had a meeting at 6pm, is there a possibility that something more important would 'come up' or is that something you would make happen no matter what? Of course you would make it happen! Unfortunately, we live in a world where we don't treat our friends and family the same way. If someone tries to flake on me, I tell them this:

'We certainly do not have to be friends, but if we are going to be friends, I need to know that you respect my time and I will respect yours as well. My time is very valuable to me, what became more important to you than respecting the plans we had made?'

From a place of Radical Belief, I firmly believe that what I bring to the table is more important than anything that could possibly 'come up.' If someone chooses not to see the value in spending time with me, that's okay, but that's also not someone I choose to keep in my space.

In my life, sometimes things come up, and I am committed to jumping through hoops and going leaps and bounds to being in integrity with the things that I say I'm going to do. Yes, I am an extremist, but I firmly believe that's what it takes to create the world I believe in.

I have a deep respect for my Mentor, a man named Michael Strasner. Michael has an amazing mentorship program that he was enrolling me into. We had a great conversation and I was so enrolled in what he brings to the table and told him I'm committed to being part of his next 9 month training.

He said, "Great! By when will you have the deposit?"

"By the time I go to bed tonight, my deposit will be paid."

The next day, Michael said, "Braxton, I just wanted to follow up with you and see that you paid your deposit."

I looked him dead in the eye and said, "Michael, I dream of a world where that question does not even need to be asked."

He smiled. He knew exactly what I meant by that. Of course, I paid my deposit, I said that I would so I did. I dream of a world where everyone follows through with their commitments.

One summer, when I was living in Pittsburgh, my college friend miles kept inviting me to watch his beer league softball games. I kept telling him that I was a busy man and that I wasn't about to take time out of my day to watch beer league softball games that don't matter and if he wanted to drink beer together I would make time for that. He said, "what if I make the championship game, will you come then?" "fine." I said, "if you make the championship game, I will go to that." Several weeks later, I received a text

– Hey man, remember when you said that if I made the championship game, you would come watch?

– Yes...

— Well, we made it and the game is on Thursday

— okay, I'll be there

I received this text the Monday before his game while I was in Shanghai, China and my flight wasn't going to be back until Friday evening. I very easily could have said, "Miles, I know I said I would go to your game, but I also didn't think I would be in China the same week. I'm sorry, I'll find a way to make it up to you." Miles would have completely understood and there would be no love lost. Instead, I called Air China and asked them to bump my flight up 24 hours and enrolled them in doing so for free. I made it to his game **BECAUSE I SAID I WOULD**.

Another example of this came when I was taking the leadership program for MITT. One of the rules was 'Take care of your buddy. If your buddy is late then you are late. My buddy was a guy named John Cheek. He and I were both on separate cross country road trips to make it to our first mandatory weekend for the leadership program. I was in Phoenix driving my RV with a few other friends when I received a call Tuesday morning before the weekend started from Johns coach telling me that his car was broken down in Tulsa Oklahoma and he wasn't going to make it for the weekend. Knowing that I made a commitment to take care of my buddy and if he misses the weekend then so do I, i got a rental car and drove from Phoenix to Tulsa, quickly fixed up his van and drove all the way to Los Angeles making it just in time for the start of the mandatory training weekend because I am the type of person who goes leaps and bounds to be in integrity with the things I said I would do. **To the extent that I am willing to go to fulfill my commitments is the extent that the rest of the world is willing to go for me in achieving my vision**.

When I make powerful declarations, I don't know what mountains I may get to climb or the obstacles that I get to leap over to be true to my word, but I know for a fact that I will fight to make sure I achieve it. In the world of entrepreneurship, I place people into 3 categories

A. One who makes a powerful declaration and follows through in both letter and in spirit to make it happen

B. One who over promises and under delivers. These people intend on being their word and seeing things through but cut corners and stop when they don't believe there is possibility to continue on. Most people fall into this category. Most people, by definition, are average

C. A flat out liar

Having the power to make a declaration such that the people around me are fully enrolled by what I'm saying is a huge responsibility. I watched the Fyre music festival documentary on Netflix and as I watched it, I heavily related with the main character, Billy McFarland. I have the exact same set of skills that Billy has. I have the ability to dream big and powerfully declare a vision such that everyone in the room is bought in by the mission I am pursuing. The key to success in entrepreneurship isn't doing the things in excellence only when the task is being pursued. It also involves being in excellence when the goal isn't being pursued. What do I mean by this? Very simple. If you want to know how someone is successful, watch him or her when he or she is not working. That will give a very strong indicator of the habits he or she is creating. Do they hit the snooze button? Do they make their beds in the morning? Do they go to the gym? Do they eat healthy? I would argue that these factors are more important than the things they do at work in the pursuit of success. Something j used to do when I was working with Southwestern was jump out of bed and run into a freezing cold shower. This was an exceptionally hard decision to make and when I do this, I train myself to go off automatic and make the growth based decisions. My morning sets the tone for the rest of my day. I form the habit of training my mind to take the road less traveled by. Successful people form the habit of doing what failures don't want to do. Success doesn't happen when I feel like it. My vision isn't going to manifest if I only pursue it when it is convenient for me. There will be times where I am downright embedded in the deepest amounts of feelings and emotions and I still get to choose my vision. I still get to create results. **To the extent that I am willing to push through my feelings is the extent that I achieve the life of my dreams**.

BOOK OF BRAXTON

CHAPTER 2

LISTEN TO WHAT'S
IMPORTANT TO THEM

"Nobody cares how much you know until
they know how much you care."

—Anonymous

In July of 2019, I visited Medellin, Colombia on a vacation with my friend Micaiah where the national language is Spanish. Hardly anyone we met in Medellin spoke any English, and Micaiah speaks practically no Spanish. I grew up learning Spanish and have taken effort over the past few years to learn as my ex girlfriend was Mexican and some of her family members don't speak English. In order to communicate with the people down there, we relied on Google translate and my limited knowledge of the language.

To my surprise, people gravitated towards me. They were fascinated: a white man who knows our language! I thought about it for a minute. The culture we have created in America frowns upon people who visit our country and don't know our language (though America doesn't actually have a national language). The effective attitude we have towards people is: if you want to live here, you have to either get by or learn.

We of course could use Google translate and communicate quite easily with the people and understand and exactly what was being said, but in my experience, for them, it took away from the authenticity of the connection. Google translate certainly didn't 'devalue' anything, but the natural dialogue added an extra layer of authenticity—it showed a level of care that subtly opened them up to trusting and connecting.

I'm sure you've heard someone say, "God gave us 2 ears and one mouth for a reason." Listening is the most powerful tool in communication. There are so many levels of listening that we can practice and people communicate in dozens of different ways. The individual words that are coming out of one's mouth is only a fraction to what they're really saying and if you aren't present to the other gestures, you may very well miss the bigger picture. Facial features, voice tone, body language are all extremely important when it comes to active listening.

When I'm in conversation, and someone thanks me for my time or thanks me for connecting with them, I always respond, "I didn't have anything better to do. I want to be clear though. It's not that I'm not busy because I absolutely have plenty of things that I could be doing right now. I just firmly believe that there is nothing on this Earth that is better for me to do than to connect with one of my fellow human beings on this journey of life." I mean that. It's genuine and people feel cared about.

"Easy reading is damn hard writing."

—Nathan Hawthorne

I read this in a book and it got me thinking. Going back to my overall vision that everyone matters, I truly believe that each person is equally valuable on this earth. When I choose to see each person for the infinitely beautiful being that they are, I can look past their walls, into their greatness and hear the powerful message they were born to tell. Every single person on this Earth matters. Not one person is any more significant than the next. It is natural to gravitate towards those who are communicating in a way that is easy to understand, but when the layers are uncovered and the work is done, there is equal value in those whose communication isn't quite as clear. This is where active listening is extremely important. When I listen to what each person is saying and I see them for their greatness, there is no hierarchy of significance as we are all equal in our uniqueness. Love each other, and listen to what your neighbor is trying to communicate. You just might learn something.

Lester knew to go there because he was an incredible active listener. I never said anything about my real status but he was both listening to what I was saying AND what I was not saying. It's also the biggest reason why he was able to score such a beautiful woman to be his wife. People want to feel heard and understood and nobody in my life has done that better than Lester Crafton.

Part of active listening is caring enough about someone to call them forth and interrupt the pattern. One day, I picked up the phone and called my old college roommate. I asked him,

"What have you been searching for your entire life that you haven't yet found?"

"Well that's easy, the love of a beautiful woman." He responded

"Can I asked you something? What are your daily habits like?"

"Well, I typically wake up and go teach, during baseball season, I go and coach. Then I come home drink a couple of beers and watch some TV."

"Well, if you're really looking for that relationship, how are those habits in congruence with what you say you really want? If I told you that I had access to something that could truly get you to that place, is that something you would be interested in?"

"Of course…"

Enrollment is about the other person. Let me say that again ENROLLMENT IS ABOUT THE OTHER PERSON!!!!!!!!! If I am enrolling someone into something, it is crucial that I listen to him/her and know what he/she really wants. What I want for them is irrelevant if it has nothing to do with what he/she is looking for. **To the extent that I listen to the person I'm enrolling and care enough about him/her to paint that vision into life is the effectiveness I become as an enroller.**

A friend of mine called me up one day for coaching on growing her business. I listened to what she was saying and answered back by pouring my heart into her. I could tell that she was caught up in the mechanics on 'how' to do it, so I made a point to be fully present with her and completely open and vulnerable. In the middle of my speaking, she stopped me and said, 'wow! That's a great line, I'm going to write that down.'

I screamed back, 'YOU'RE MISSING THE ENTIRE POINT!!!! IT HAS NOTHING TO DO WITH THE

WORDS!! I realize that my words are brilliant and eloquently articulated, but that is only because I'm fully present with you. If I were trying to sound one way or another then it wouldn't translate. Focus on how I'm being with you right now and exchange *that* into your enrollments.'

It's never about the words. It's 100% about the being. I watched my friend Olivia--one of the most powerful women I have ever met--coach a man in Spanish. Hablo poco Español. She was present with him and she truly cared about him. She was passionate and graceful. Everyone in the room felt the power and connection between the two of them though we hardly understood a single word. We were all moved by her way of being with him. That is where the work is done.

It is very common to get caught up into personal agenda—hell I've done it 1,000,000 times. The beauty is, when I choose to go back into active listening, the person will tell me why I'm being ineffective. If I'm operating on my personal agenda, they will say something like "that sounds great for you, but it doesn't seem like that's something I'd be into." This is them effectively saying, "I don't want what you have." It is the result of not listening to what THEY want. I can't stress it enough **ENROLLMENT IS ABOUT THE OTHER PERSON AND WHAT HE/SHE WANTS**. When you connect with their deepest desires and focus on what they really want and created it bigger than they have ever seen and make it more real than they've ever experienced, they will follow you anywhere. The irony in everything is this: **when I let go of the mechanics on 'how' to do it, and focus on being present, I manifest my intention.**

BOOK OF BRAXTON

CHAPTER 3

MEET THEM WHERE THEY ARE

"A leader is someone who holds her- or himself accountable for finding the potential in people and processes."

— Brené Brown

Intimacy is something that is grown, and when it comes to trust, we are all at different places in our journey. In relatability and enrollment, it is crucial to meet the person where they are. What does this mean? The first thing that comes to mind is empathizing. Never make a person wrong for the way he/she is behaving. Relate with them. Understand how they got to that place and support him/her and safely revisiting the event and painting a new meaning for what happened.

We as human beings are meaning making machines and our perception is our reality. The story is in the telling. The only thing that is real is the present, that's why it's called the reality. I choose to be the author of my own life. I believe that every single interaction is both a blessing and a gift. Sometimes in life, the greatest gifts in life can be the most difficult to receive because they are typically buried under the deepest amounts of pain.

In this society, it has become standard to become victim to other people or unfortunate events. Any time I find myself in a situation like this, I ask myself, 'Did a bad person do a bad thing to me? OR Did an amazing person show me a valuable lesson on how I'm showing up in life?' The Law of Attraction is beautiful and powerful. When I come from the place that I am the author of my life and people are messengers who simply show me how I'm showing up, I view things from a place of empowerment. Tony Robbins says, "Life happens for me, not to me.'

When I go back and visit the past from a place of ownership and come from responsibility that I created and caused everything in my life, it puts me in the driver's seat. I am responsible for everything and anything that's ever happened in my life. We attract things into our lives for a reason. Choosing to forgive the other person and taking ownership of what happens creates peace and freedom. Nobody has done anything 'to me' they have simply reflected back to me my ways of being that operate at a lower frequency.

The most painful moment in my life happened in the summer of 2018. A girl who I was interested in accused me of rape after we had what I believed to be completely consensual sex. For months after that, I found myself playing victim to her behavior. The voice inside my head kept saying, "I didn't do anything wrong…" "Why would someone do that?" The more power I gave to that voice, the worse I felt. The worst part is that I believed that she believed her story. Even worse, in the world of the #BelieveAllWomen and #MeToo movement, I didn't tell anyone because I didn't think anyone would believe me. I kept all of this inside and it was tearing me apart to the point that it nearly killed me. Thoughts of suicide ran through my head daily. As each day went by the closer these thoughts came to becoming reality. I was in a deep amount of grief and pain until one day, it hit me and I chose to be in ownership and look at it from a place of full responsibility. After all, life happens for me, not to me. For the first time in my life, I asked myself the question: Did a bad person do a bad thing to me, or did an amazing person show me a valuable lesson on how I was showing up? While I didn't do anything wrong, I totally see the lesson here. For a long time, I carried weight that wasn't mine. I had created a habit with people to put their weight off on me. This amazing woman taught me not to carry weight that wasn't mine. When I do, I form the habit to make myself a martyr. To me, it was a tough way to learn the consequences of letting other people put things off on me. **When I choose to be the author of my life, I create empowerment through being in ownership of everything that happens. If I see how I caused it, I can make a change in my life and create a different result in the future.**

"Father forgive them, for they know not what they do."

—Jesus Christ

I always hear talks about unconditional love. To me, the above quote from Jesus really sums it up. This is why Jesus is the most badass person in history. People are literally crucifying him for absolutely no reason and he still has the heart to love them and ask for forgiveness. I see posts all of the time on Facebook about getting rid of all of the 'Toxic' people in life. I CANNOT STRESS THIS ENOUGH. I invite you to drop the notion that there are 'Toxic' people on this planet. People are not Toxic. All people are amazing and beautiful born to love and be loved. As I grow and transform, toxic people have left my life not because I chose to write them off and 'get rid of them,' but because the space that I have held for them and the way that I view them has changed giving them the space to drop their walls that I once perceived as Toxic and stand as their authentic loving self. The way people show up to me is simply feedback for the space that I'm holding for them and in creating a world where everyone knows they matter and feels loved, it is up to me to receive the feedback and transform my ways of being to reach the hearts of the people in my life. Nobody is 'Toxic' they are simply providing me with information on where I get to go to support them in reaching a world that works for everyone.

Any time someone does something that triggers me, I've trained my brain to think, "Wow! What a blessing. Someone so amazing just showed me something that brought up a feeling of pain and now I have an incredible opportunity to dive in and find the root of the feeling and change my interpretation of the event to give different meaning to the story I'm making up about it to create a reality worth living in." I find that response creates a much more peaceful reality for myself than thinking, "What a dick! I'm never talking to him again because he triggers me!"

Nothing bad has ever happened to me in my entire life. It's not that unpleasant events haven't taken place in my life. I have just actively chooses to take these unpleasant events on and choose to see how they were all such a blessing. This is where the healing begins. The healing begins when we choose to forgive and see everything as a blessing and choose to see how it was such a gift. Everything that happens is a gift if we choose to see it. You can be right about whatever you choose to be right about. The question is, which interpretation gives you the most power to be the author of your life?

CHAPTER 4

HOLD YOURSELF AND
OTHERS HIGH

"As a leader, it's a major responsibility on your shoulders to practice the behavior you want others to follow."

— Himanshu Bhatia, founder, Rose International.

For years and years, I have been told to use my voice and to speak up, and for years and years, I did when it was on behalf of someone else. After all, my vision is to create a world where everyone knows they matter, and I have been committed to standing for everyone in my life. What I didn't realize is that I am part of everyone. It's been so easy for me to speak for everyone, but up until now, I haven't spoken for myself. In doing this, I was neither holding myself or others to their highest self. When I allow others to break their word with me, I am neither holding myself nor the person who broke their commitment with me high. It doesn't matter to me what you're committed to, but what matters that I do the things that I say I'm going to do.

I had a mentor and a good friend take time out of his life to grow me to my best self. I was honored that he saw me for my absolute greatness and took time out of his life to support me in living my best life. I was working with him and deep down, I knew I was slacking on my commitments so I began to avoid him (even though I knew he had the key to getting me back on track). I ran into him at a social event and he walked up to me and put his arm around me and said, 'Bro, I know you've been avoiding me.' This opened the door for a really in depth coaching opportunity about how I was showing up and what had me avoid.

Because Garrain had the courage to call me forth when I was avoiding, it opened up the door for what I realized: how I was acting towards leadership is exactly how people who i was leading was acting towards me. We are balls of energy. Going back to Newton's 3rd law: For every action, there is an equal and opposite reaction. **To the extent that I show up to others is the extent that others will show up to me**.

I had a friend named Arjun that I invited to join Herb-aLife nutrition with me. I had just started my health and fitness journey and had already created results in my body transformation, and he said he wanted to join me. After 6 weeks, he was still talking about how he was excited to sign up and use the platform as an opportunity to make a difference in people's lives. He is in finance and called me one day for coaching on his business and asked, "How do I grow my business? People keep telling me that they want to sign up but they never take action. How do I create the urgency for them to enroll?"

I said, "Are you open for me pointing something out?" (In coaching it is extremely important and more effective when I request permission before digging in)

He said, "Of course."

I said, "If you want to create urgency and holding people to their word, you get to do that first. You've been telling me that you wanted to sign up in my business for weeks and I'm going to hold you to that. **To the extent that you lack urgency when you say you're going to do something is the extent that people will lack urgency when you ask them to do something.**"

His response (sarcastic of course): "Stop making sense bro!! It's killing me and forcing me to make choices!"

One time, a friend asked me for support because she was going through a tough time financially. I asked her how I could support her. She told me that $1,000 would really help. I told her that if I gave her $1,000, I would be robbing her of learning the skill set to earn it herself. When it comes to holding others high, always take the road less traveled by and inspire them to stretch. In this case, I absolutely could have given her $1,000, but that would have been disempowering and enabling. What that communicates is: here you go. I don't believe you are capable of earning on your own so I am going to give something to you because I am capable. It's effectively saying 'I'm better than you.'

In my experience, it's just how the world works and to me makes it both simple and beautiful. When I'm in integrity, people are in integrity with me. It's how I let go of grudges and choose forgiveness every single time. I understand how the world works. I understand that the energy that I'm receiving came from the energy that I'm giving out. I am the author of my own life and I choose unlimited power and omnipotence. I choose to be fully responsible. Whatever we believe to be true WILL BE TRUE. Why not choose to believe the most empowering interpretation of every event?

BOOK OF BRAXTON

CHAPTER 5

THE POWER OF CHARISMA

"We're here for a reason. I believe a bit of the reason is to throw little torches out to lead people through the dark."

— Whoopi Goldberg

To me, charisma is directly related to unattachment. When someone is completely unattached to the result and focused on doing his/her best-- people follow that. Another important part of charisma is standing for something rather than standing against something. What we resist, persists. I hear these catch phrases all of the time. I've heard them for years and years, but only recently did I truly understand what that means. Mother Theresea taught me exactly what it means though. She said, "I was once asked why I don't participate in anti-war demonstrations. I said that I will never do that. But as soon as you have a pro peace rally, I'll be there."

My question for you: where in your life have you been holding an anti-war rally instead of a pro peace rally? How has that been working for you? I coach people on manifesting relationships (I have absolutely done this myself). All of the time I hear: 'I want someone loving, someone I can trust, someone who isn't controlling or manipulative, etc.' The human brain is programmed to gravitate towards familiarity. When you meet someone who is loving, trustworthy, controlling and manipulative, your brain will recognize it as familiar and you will become attracted to that person. I always ask, what is on the other side of control and manipulation? They will say surredorous, open, compassionate, committed, etc. Sostart looking for those things.

This is another phrase that I heard over and over and over again. Sometimes people say these quotes that are incredible deep and impactful, but they become overused and cliche that they lose their meaning, and they don't effectively resonate. Upon digging deeper and finding meaning, this quote remains true. Again, who is enrollment about?

Andrew Carnegie is a powerful example of charisma. He became one of the wealthiest people in human history. When he was at the peak of his wealth in 1901, he was worth about $380 Million BACK THEN! With inflation, that is the equivalent of $309 Billion. For Context, the 3 wealthiest people today are Jeff Bezos, Warren Buffet and Bill Gates. Andrew Carnegie was worth more money than the 3 of them... COMBINED!!

How did he become so wealthy? He was the founder of Carnegie Steel and made his money in Pittsburgh, PA using the city's 3 waterways to his advantage by producing steel and shipping it across the country. Though he was the head of Carnegie Steel, he knew next to nothing about steel. What he knew was how to get the right people next to each other in the right room. Andrew was a master enroller. He paid people what they were worth and they delivered for him. He had a servant's heart. When he retired at age 66, **HE GAVE ALL OF HIS MONEY AWAY!** People surrounded by Andrew knew that he genuinely cared, and his actions showed. He believed in creating value and bringing out the best in people and they followed him wherever he went.

When I genuinely care about someone and am fully present with what they are up to, they feel it. When I come from a place of pure compassion and genuine care, leadership emerges. I was born and raised Christian (hence all of the Bible quotes throughout this reading) and have fallen in love with the message of Jesus Christ. Over the years, I have opened my eyes to many other practices as well. I have studied Hinduism, Taoism, and Buddhism and I have attended Tony Robbins' Cult as well as Mastery in Transformational Training and have adapted the philosophies of each of these practices into my life. My mom, who is also a devout Christian, was asking why I studied so many practices when "The way, the truth and the life" is Jesus' message. I asked her what the mission of Christianity is. She said it was to share the message of Jesus Christ. I asked her how she would do that if she met someone who practiced Hinduism.

"Well, I would tell this person about Jesus."

"What if this person wants to tell you about Krishna?" I replied.

"Well, I believe that Jesus Christ is the one true way to heaven."

"What if this person believes that everyone should strive to achieve dharma and that their souls are immortal and will be reincarnated upon death? Are you going to make this person wrong about what he/she believes in order to attempt to enroll him/her into your belief? Good luck…"

What I have found is that when I connect on what is important to them first, they are much more open to what is important to me when I choose to share. If I am an expert on Hinduism and I first listen to the person about his/her beliefs and share what I know about Hinduism, when it comes time to talk about Christianity and the message of Jesus Christ, he/she will be wide open to listen. "Nobody cares how much you know until they know how much you care."

Charisma is one of those things that gets to be handled with extreme care as there are consequences to being a charismatic leader. I always give the 3 options when I enroll because giving choice 3 allows someone to point out something to me and help me see what I may not be seeing (choice 3: enroll me on why proceeding another direction better serves the overall vision). I trust myself to hold steadfast to what I believe is the most world serving direction, but there are certainly times where I have proceeded believing that to be true, acquiring a huge following to find out that I have led them into a trap. That sucks! And that is why leadership is challenging and takes courage. The questions I ask myself is this: does this serve all parties? Does this move everyone involved forward? Is there a win for everyone involved?

CHAPTER 6

HOW TO WIN THE TRUST OF OTHERS

"Leadership is not a person or a position. It is a complex moral relationship between people based on trust, obligation, commitment, emotion, and a shared vision of the good."

— **Joanne B. Ciulla**

What I have found, everything in relationships comes down to trust. To me, trust is the most important thing in cultivating a relationship. It's my highest value. I say it all the time to girls when I first begin to date: "I can't promise that I won't hurt you—because I will—I'm a human being. What I can promise is that I will

always be man enough to stick around and clean it up."
It's real. It's vulnerable. It's open.

When it comes to earning someone's trust, it comes down
to caring enough about them to be honest. It's about sharing what's on my heart at any given time and showing my
cards especially when I'm afraid to do so.

In sales, I've always been told to say the prospect's objec-
tion before they have a chance to say it. Put it out in the
open and cover it before they do. When it comes out of
my mouth first, it has no power when they say it later.
Same things goes in relationships and enrollment.

When I'm enrolling someone into my following, I first
ask them 'do you trust me.' For some people, this can be a
tough question to ask because many people are afraid that
someone will say no (they really never do). Most people
won't tell you to your face that they don't trust you. They
will say something like 'I totally trust you, I just don't
trust *them.'* As if *them* is something outside of you. If I'm
enrolling someone into something, whatever it may be, is
an extension of me. There is no *them* there is only me and
the person who I'm enrolling. Saying that they don't trust
them is a cop out and a back door. It's an avoidance of digging deep and working through the real issue.

Trust is very important because whatever experience the
person who I'm enrolling has of me is the exact experience they will have in whatever I'm enrolling them into.

To me, it's very important that we have a phenomenal, trusting relationship because I genuinely want everyone to have the best experience they possibly can.

"If you trust me—go—I promise you will have a powerful experience and you will grow exponentially from it and our relationship will become more intimate as we connect on the same language. If you don't trust me, that's okay. I care about you and I care enough to work through it with you. I'm not a mind reader. If there's a lack of trust, I invite you to develop it with me, so we can create something new."

When I care enough to consistently stand for connection, people sense the genuine care and feel safe to open up. In my experience, the bigger the issue we work through, the closer we become when the issue is resolved. **When my intention is creating trust, the other person feels safe. They see that, they feel that, and intimacy is created. To the extent that I'm willing to go with the person to open my heart is the extent that they will be willing to surrender to me and open their hearts.** This is especially important in cultivating a relationship with my life partner. I want a relationship of full transparency. I want a relationship where I can share everything and be fully received when I do. I am not perfect by any means of the stretch nor is anyone reading this. When I open my heart and create the space to show my imperfections,

I show that I trust. In order to be trusted by others, I must first show that I trust them.

Have you ever heard anyone say you must first give to get. In creating trust and openness, it works the same way. In order for someone to share with me, I must first go out on a limb and share with them. Intimacy is beautiful and sharing secrets creates connection. The deeper we go with each other, the more intimacy is created. When we are intimately connected, the height of attraction is reached.

CONCLUSION

Quote: "If you don't sacrifice for what you want, what you want will be the sacrifice."

We live in a world where people show a façade. What I see for my life is showing every part of me and trusting that I am fully received for my authentic self. It's easy to be received for the façade; it takes courage to show the darkest parts of my soul. If I'm creating an authentic relationship with another person, they get to know the battles I am facing and what I am working through. When they know my battles, they can support me; and when I know what they are facing, I can support them. No judgement, just two imperfect beings sharing with each other what's raw. What's real. Nobody on this planet is perfect. The invitation is to show the not so pretty sides of yourself so that the other person feels safe to do the same with you.

I found the 'give to get' mentality show up in the professional world as well. When it comes to investing in myself,

I have taken major strides over the past few years. I spent $15,000 to go to several Tony Robbins courses, I've taken every single MITT course available (totally about $15,000 as well), and I have invested a decent chunk of money in HerbaLife products for my health. After I bought the Tony Robbins package, someone said to me,

"Holy crap! Braxton Benson Franklin Amundson! That is a lot of money! Why would you spend that much money?"

I said, "Because I want to hang out with people who don't think it's a lot of money."

If I look at $15k as 'a lot of money' that's all it will ever be. Millionaires look at it as a reasonable investment in themselves. When I surround myself with that mindset, I, too, will create the space to break my financial belief barriers. If I'm looking for an investment in me, I get to take the step in first investing in myself.

When I invest in myself, I am telling myself "I'm worth it." I trust myself to create the value in what I am doing.' Lots of times its one of the toughest investments for one to make. The question I would ask someone resistant to do so is this: if you are building towards something bigger than yourself, you are going to need people to work with you. You are effectively going to be asking them for their time and their money. If you are resistant to investing into yourself, why should anyone else choose to invest in you? **When you decide that you are worth it, the universe always responds.**